Reading Strategies That Work

Helping Young Readers
Develop Independent Reading Skills

Written by Jo Fitzpatrick

Editor: Karen P. Hall

Illustrator: Ann Iosa

Project Director: Carolea Williams

 © 1998 Creative Teaching Press, Inc., Cypress, CA 90630

Table of Contents

Activities for Early-Fluent and Fluent Readers

Introduction

Educators, researchers, and hundreds of "inquiring minds" have been extensively investigating the factors that influence success or failure in the beginning reading process. The big quest has been to determine what efficient readers do that inefficient readers do not.

Studies show that many inefficient readers lack the techniques or "strategies" needed to read unfamiliar words in print. They are unable to detect and correct blatant mistakes that affect comprehension and meaning. They also show an over-reliance on graphophonic cueing (sounding out words). At the same time, these same students are given fewer opportunities to use reading strategies independently. The very students who need to freely explore and experiment with a variety of reading materials are often limited to guided drill-and-practice instruction.

All students can benefit from learning and using reading strategies—simple "tricks" for decoding text. The goal of *Reading Strategies That Work* is to provide students with the necessary techniques to help them identify and read challenging words in print. Included in this resource are a variety of practical, simple-to-use activities that reinforce the use of reading strategies; reproducibles and word lists to use with the activities; culminating activities that encourage students to self-monitor and assess their use of reading strategies; and suggestions for parent involvement in the reading process. *Reading Strategies That Work* also provides a reproducible bookmark that includes "picture prompts" to remind students of different reading strategies to use as they read independently.

The strategies in this book will help develop readers who

- are both independent and strategic.
- increase their reading ability each time they interact with text.
- automatically search for meaning as they read.

As students use reading strategies, they will learn

- how prior knowledge and experiences support the reading process.
- how context clues assist comprehension and decoding.
- how letter patterns and word structure facilitate "word attack."
- how and when to use phonetic clues.

The Reading Process

Learning to read is a complex process that requires more than just looking at letters on a page. It requires a person to recognize written symbols (letters of the alphabet), associate sounds to symbols, blend sounds to form distinct units (words), organize the units into strands (sentences), and translate the strands into a coherent and meaningful message. To read successfully, a child must master the following skills:

Visual Scanning

Recognizing individual letters, letter order, and whole words.

Sounding Out

Matching distinct sounds to written symbols, and combining those sounds and symbols together to form words.

Analyzing Sentence Structure

Using rules of grammar, mechanics, and spelling to connect words to form sentences.

Deriving Meaning from Text

Relying on prior knowledge and real-life experiences to see and understand the written message.

Learning to read is not an automatic process—it must be taught. Children need practice looking at, listening to, and deriving meaning from words. They need to understand how a message they say aloud can be communicated through symbols on paper.

Successful readers use a variety of techniques or "reading strategies" to help them scan text, sound out letters, analyze sentence structure, and "translate" the sentences into a meaningful message. These strategies can be grouped into three distinct categories or "cueing systems"—semantic, syntactic, and graphophonic.

Semantic Strategies

Children "read for meaning" and identify unfamiliar words by

- using clues in the pictures and in the context of the story (picture clues, context clues).
- comparing what they are reading to what they already know (prior knowledge).

Syntactic Strategies

Children study sentence structure and identify unfamiliar words by

- looking at verb tense and subject-verb agreement (grammar).
- attending to predictable language patterns in written text (grammar).

Graphophonic Strategies

Children associate spoken sounds with printed letters. They identify unfamiliar words by

- sounding out individual letters and letter combinations (letter sounds).
- looking at letter sequence and "chunks" of the word (letter patterns).

Semantic, syntactic, and graphophonic strategies are interdependent. When a child reads, he or she usually relies on more than one cueing system at a time. Consider the following sentence:

I can read a book.

If a child is unfamiliar with the underlined word, he or she can use semantic strategies (context clues, prior knowledge) to identify the word as *read*. However, one can also *make* a book, *drop* a book, *cover* a book, and so on. By using graphophonic strategies to "sound out" the letter *r,* the child has a better chance of identifying the word correctly.

But what about the following example:

Yesterday I read a book.

Semantic and graphophonic strategies are not enough. Syntactic cues are also needed to identify the word as past tense and to pronounce it correctly— */red/* instead of */reed/.*

Beginning readers must be able to use all three cueing systems in a coordinated way. By cross-checking cues as they read, students confirm their understanding and gain competence in all three areas.

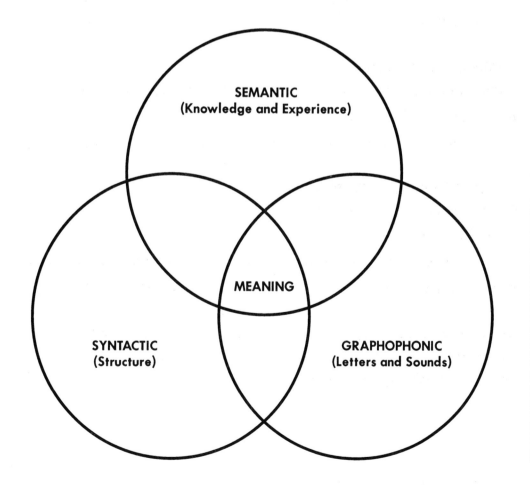

Teaching Reading Strategies

Teaching reading strategies should begin long before children actually learn to read. Before children can decode printed words, they need to be familiar with letter sounds; to understand printed words, children need to associate words to real-life people, places, and things.

When teaching reading strategies to your class, provide many opportunities for students to see, hear, experience, and discuss the world around them. Make language development and vocabulary practice an ongoing process. Include read-alouds, storytelling, and group discussions as part of your daily routine. Encourage students to listen to and explore letter sounds as they read words aloud—the ability to hear and manipulate letter sounds in spoken language (phonemic awareness) will help your students read and understand printed text.

The activities in this resource will help you teach reading strategies to students at different reading levels—pre-emergent readers (see pages 24-37), emergent readers (see pages 38-59), and early-fluent/fluent readers (see pages 60-84). Keep in mind that some of your fluent readers may benefit from completing basic activities offered in the pre-emergent and emergent sections before they attempt more challenging exercises. When choosing reading materials to use with the activities, select slightly advanced text so that students have enough (but not too many) challenging words with which to practice their skills. As their abilities improve, use the culminating activities (pages 85-86) to help students self-monitor and assess their use of reading strategies.

Before asking students to complete any activity, model how to use the appropriate reading strategies. (Note that each activity page indicates the reading strategies being reinforced. Also refer to the Strategy Chart on pages 22-23.) Think aloud as you decode a word or search for important details in the story. Invite students to "play teacher" and talk you through the thinking process. Focus on one or two strategies at a time, depending on students' individual needs or reading abilities. Model and practice the strategies as a class or in small groups before having students work independently.

You may choose to have students focus on simple fill-in-the-blank exercises before teaching them more challenging activities. This will help students become familiar with reading strategies in a simple, straight-forward format. Create a variety of fill-in-the-blank exercises using the reproducible Mystery-Word Activity sheet on page 11 and Mystery-Word Sentences on page 12. (See *Using Bookmark Picture Prompts*, pages 13-17, for an explanation of the graphics at the bottom of the reproducible page.) Photocopy the sheet and write a Mystery-Word sentence on the appropriate line. Distribute copies of the page to students and complete the activity together. To extend learning, encourage students to complete Mystery-Word activities at home each week. (See *Mystery-Word Activities* in the *Parent Involvement* section, pages 18-21.)

Keep in mind that students will need continuous instruction and plenty of practice to consistently recognize and apply reading strategies. As you teach children reading strategies, consider the following suggestions:

- Select strategies based on student need and performance.

- Make instruction three-dimensional so students see how to use, when to use, and why it is important to use the strategies.

- Use text and stories from your own reading materials to teach reading strategies. The activities provided in this resource should be integrated into your current reading program.

- Have students verbalize how to use strategies before applying their knowledge to print.

- Continually model and verbalize the strategies in authentic reading situations. This is a critical step in helping students successfully learn and apply reading strategies.

- After students are familiar with reading strategies, encourage them to use more than one strategy at a time. Remember that semantic, syntactic, and graphophonic strategies are naturally interdependent.

- Allow plenty of opportunities for independent practice and application.

Mystery-Word Activity

Sentence: _____

What is the missing word? _____

Which reading strategy(s) did you use to guess the missing word? Cut
out the picture(s) that matches your answer and paste it inside the box.

Write a new sentence that contains the word.

_____

✂️ -

Mystery-Word Sentences

Use these sentences along with the Mystery-Word Activity reproducible (page 11) to make activity sheets for students to complete in class or at home. (Note that the answers and the bookmark graphics given below are for teacher use only.)

1. The teacher was _____ a song on the piano. *(playing)*

2. At school I like to sit by my f__end. *(friend)*

3. We go to school to l_____. *(learn)*

4. I like to (paint or draw?) with my pencil. *(draw)*

5. At recess we p_____ outside. *(play)*

6. Today I made a _____ out of clay. *(anything that makes sense)*

7. Our teacher likes to _____ songs every day. *(teach or sing)*

8. Listen to me say the letters of the _____. *(alphabet)*

9. The boy played with the __oy. *(toy)*

10. The number six comes after the number _____. *(five)*

11. My mom bought me a new back_____ for school. *(backpack)*

12. The school bell r_____ when it was time to go home. *(rang)*

13. My friend dressed up as a black c__t for Halloween. *(cat)*

14. I have a mane and I roar. What am I? *(lion)*

15. The Pilgrims came to America on a sh__p called the *Mayflower. (ship)*

Reading Strategies That Work © 1998 Creative Teaching Press

Using Bookmark Picture Prompts

Learning the "rules of reading" can be difficult for young readers, especially if the techniques are presented in a random, haphazard manner. An easy and effective way to help children remember and use reading strategies is through graphic reminders, or "picture prompts." Included in this resource (page 17) is a handy reproducible bookmark displaying picture prompts that correspond to different reading strategies. Your students will enjoy and benefit from using these bookmarks as they learn to read. Note that bookmark graphics are shown at the top of each activity sheet (pages 24-86) to indicate which reading strategies are being reinforced.

Understanding Bookmark Graphics

The following guidelines describe each bookmark picture prompt and how the graphic relates to different reading strategies. Use the verbal prompts and the suggested questions in the guidelines to help you introduce and discuss the illustrations with your students. When teaching the activities, emphasize the reading strategies to use and the bookmark picture prompts to refer to. After the class has been introduced to the picture prompts and received sufficient guidance using the reading strategies, encourage students to refer to their bookmarks as they read independently.

Note: Because of the interdependent nature of reading strategies (see *The Reading Process,* pages 5-7), some picture prompts represent a combination of different techniques. For example, the suggestion to "search for similarities" incorporates the use of three different strategies—looking at letter patterns, listening to letter sounds, and applying knowledge of grammar.

Guidelines for Bookmark Pictures

State the verbal prompts aloud to identify bookmark pictures to students. Use the discussion suggestions to help explain the reading strategies associated with each illustration.

Verbal Prompt: Does it make sense?

- prior knowledge (semantic strategy)

Discussion

Think about what you've read so far and what you already know about the subject. What do you think the word might be? Does the word make sense in the sentence?

Verbal Prompt: Look for key clues.

- context clues (semantic strategy)
- picture clues (semantic strategy)

Discussion

Look for key words in the sentence (nouns and descriptive words) or clues in the pictures that may help you identify an unfamiliar word.

Reading Strategies That Work © 1998 Creative Teaching Press

Verbal Prompt: Listen to how it sounds.

- letter sounds (graphophonic strategy)
- grammar (syntactic strategy)

Discussion

What are the beginning, middle, and ending sounds of the word? Sounding out the letters can help you identify the word. Guess the word and say it in the sentence. Does it sound right?

Verbal Prompt: Look for little words in big words.

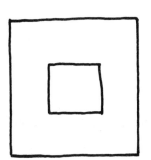

- letter patterns (graphophonic strategy)

Discussion

Look for "hidden" words first to help you pronounce and identify the larger, unfamiliar words. For example, what is the little word in sit? (it)

Verbal Prompt: Search for similarities.

- letter patterns (graphophonic strategy)
- letter sounds (graphophonic strategy)
- grammar (syntactic strategy)

Discussion

Look and listen for similarities among words. Do they rhyme? Do they have the same letter patterns?

Verbal Prompt: Try a popper.

- letter sounds (graphophonic strategy)
- context clues (semantic strategy)

Discussion

Sound out the first letter of an unfamiliar word and then continue reading the rest of the sentence. Many times the word will simply pop into your head.

Verbal Prompt: Backtrack and read again.

- prior knowledge (semantic strategy)
- context clues (semantic strategy)

Discussion

If you run across a word you don't know, go back and read the sentence again. You may notice clues you missed the first time.

Verbal Prompt: Skip it and go on.

- context clues (semantic strategy)

Discussion

If you run across a word you don't know, continue reading the sentence. Sometimes the information that follows can help you identify the unfamiliar word.

Reading Strategies That Work © 1998 Creative Teaching Press

Bookmarks

Parent Involvement

Parents play a key role in the development of reading skills in young children. They help provide critical background knowledge and real-life experiences that beginning readers need in decoding and understanding printed text. Family discussions and storytelling also help create excitement and enthusiasm for both spoken and written language.

Introducing Parents to Reading Strategies

At the beginning of the year, invite parents to school to discuss reading strategies. Photocopy and share the following example to illustrate the difficulty of reading and understanding unfamiliar print.

Τηε δογ σατ ον α λογ.

Τηε χατ σατ ιν α ηατ.

Βυτ τηε φοξ σατ βεηινδ τηε βοξ.

Explain to parents that by using different "reading strategies"—looking at the pictures, finding "clue words" in the sentences, looking at sentence structure, sounding out words, and recognizing rhyming patterns—the reader is able to translate the sentences: *The dog sat on a log. The cat sat in a hat. But the fox sat behind the box.*

After sharing the example with parents, distribute photocopies of Guidelines for Bookmark Pictures (pages 14-16) and the bookmarks (page 17) and explain how each picture prompt correlates to different reading strategies. Have parents look at a textbook passage and refer to the bookmark graphics as you demonstrate how to use different reading strategies. Encourage parents to use the suggestions in Parents as Reading Partners (page 20) to practice reading strategies with their children.

Mystery-Word Activities

Send home each week a Mystery-Word Activity sheet (page 11) for students to complete with their parents. These simple fill-in-the-blank activities help students practice, apply, and discuss different reading strategies.

To prepare activity sheets for home use, select a sentence (from the Mystery-Word Sentences on page 12 or from current classroom reading materials) and write it on a photocopy of the sheet. Make photocopies of the partially filled-out sheet for students to take home and complete. Include with the first Mystery-Word activity a copy of the parent letter (page 21) and the Guidelines for Bookmark Pictures (pages 14–16) to guide parents as they practice reading strategies with their children.

Name Sam   Date 11/15

Mystery-Word Activity

Sentence: At recess we p_____ outside.

What is the missing word? play

Which reading strategy(s) did you use to guess the missing word? Cut out the picture(s) that matches your answer and paste it inside the box.

Write a new sentence that contains the word.

I like to play with my friend.

Note: Adequately practice Mystery-Word activities in class before sending the activity sheets home with students. (See *Teaching Reading Strategies,* pages 8–10.) This will allow your students to become comfortable with the activity format before practicing the procedure with their parents.

Parents as Reading Partners

Dear Parents,

Use the following suggestions to make reading an enjoyable and rewarding experience for you and your child.

- Play little word games with your child. Make up a sentence and leave out a word, for example, *I went to the doctor because I was _____.* Ask your child to tell you what the missing word should be and why.

- Before reading a book aloud, ask your child questions about the story that can be answered by looking at the pictures.

- Read poems and nursery rhymes and leave out a rhyming word. Have your child guess the missing word and explain how he or she got the answer.

- Have your child look only at the pictures of a well-illustrated book and then ask him or her to make up a story to go with them.

- As you read aloud, leave out a word from a sentence (nouns work best) and ask your child to "fill in the blank." Ask your child to identify which clues in the sentence helped him or her identify the missing word.

- As you read aloud, make a silly mistake that affects the meaning of the sentence. See if your child notices and corrects you. If not, stop reading and think aloud as you correct your mistake. This will help teach your child to self-monitor while reading.

- While reading together, have your child look at a paragraph in the story and find all the words that have a specific letter combination, for example, all words ending with *-ing.*

Happy Reading!

Reading Strategies That Work © 1998 Creative Teaching Press

Dear Parents,

Reading opens a world of excitement, creativity, and fun. But before your child can learn to read, he or she needs to understand the relationship between letter sounds and symbols. Equally important is understanding that printed words "translate" into meaningful messages.

In class, your child is learning reading strategies to help him or her decode words and read for meaning. Simple techniques include examining book illustrations, finding "clue words" in sentences, looking at sentence structure, sounding out words, and recognizing rhyming patterns. You can help your child practice these important reading skills by completing together Mystery-Word Activity sheets. Each week, a new activity sheet will be sent home for you and your child to enjoy. Complete the activity together by reading aloud the fill-in-the-blank sentence and then asking your child to

- guess the missing word.
- discuss the reading strategies used to guess the word.
- cut out the picture(s) that corresponds to the reading strategy(ies) used. (Refer to the attached sheets, *Guidelines for Bookmark Pictures.*)
- paste the picture(s) inside the box.
- help you write a new sentence containing the word.

Encourage your child to "think aloud" and explain which reading strategies he or she uses to identify the missing word. Extend learning by having your child practice reading strategies with a variety of printed materials in and around your home, such as magazines, comic books, and road signs. Your child will treasure these special times together, and you will be helping him or her become an enthusiastic, successful reader.

Happy Reading!

Strategy Chart

How to Use This Chart

The following chart shows the reading strategies used in each activity in this book. Refer to this chart when looking for activities to reinforce specific reading skills in your students

	\multicolumn{6}{c}{Strategy}					
	prior knowledge	picture clues	context clues	grammar	letter sounds	letter patterns
Pre-Emergent Readers						
Sneak a Peek	●	●				
Read a Picture	●	●				
Match 'em Up	●	●			●	
Stick 'em Up	●	●			●	
On the Road to Reading	●	●				
Lightning Flash	●	●				
Read a Rhyme	●		●		●	●
Get On with It	●	●				
Use It and Lose It	●	●			●	
Huh?	●		●	●		
Stomp It Out	●				●	
Poppers			●		●	
Pop It Out			●		●	
Stop and Say			●		●	
Emergent Readers						
Give It Meaning	●		●			
Hide and Seek	●		●			
It's Your Choice			●	●		
Ah Ha!	●		●			
Look Before You Leap	●		●			
Flip-Up Families	●				●	●
Mix and Match					●	●
Pick and Choose					●	
Blending Race					●	●
Word Staircase					●	●
I Spy					●	●
Leading Letter					●	●
Word-Family Strips	●				●	●
House of Words					●	●

| | Strategy | | | | | |
	prior knowledge	picture clues	context clues	grammar	letter sounds	letter patterns
Emergent Readers (cont.)						
Colorful Words					●	●
Rainbow Clues					●	●
Build a Word					●	●
Scavenger Hunt					●	●
Fixer-Upper	●		●	●		
Letter Snatcher	●		●		●	●
Sticky Words	●			●		
The Attribute Game	●			●	●	
Early-Fluent and Fluent Readers						
Red-Flag It	●		●	●	●	
The Missing Link	●		●			
Word Translator	●		●			
Word Associations	●				●	
Telephone Spelling	●				●	
Grab-Bag Game	●				●	
Try-ers			●		●	
Word Stretcher					●	●
Shift and Change					●	●
Super Sleuth					●	●
Guess My Word	●				●	
Peek-a-Boo Clue	●		●			
Be the Sentence	●			●		
Skim and Scan	●		●			
Hieroglyphics	●		●			
Backtrack	●		●			
Instant Replay	●		●			
It's Time	●		●			
Computer Mix-Up	●		●	●		
Look-and-Listen Directories					●	●
Fun with Directories			●	●	●	
Roll a Word	●				●	●
A Phrase That Pays	●		●		●	●

 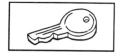

Sneak a Peek

Materials

- picture book
- piece of construction paper
- Sneak a Peek sheet (page 87)

Reading Strategies

▶ Using **prior knowledge** to add meaning to text

▶ Looking at **picture clues** to predict story content

Select a picture book (one students are unfamiliar with) and read the title aloud. Show each page of the book and have students look at the illustrations to "preview" the story. (Cover the text with construction paper.) Model how to look for key clues in the pictures to predict what is happening in the story. Think aloud as you discuss the illustrations. Ask questions that will help students examine each picture carefully, such as *Who is in the picture? What is happening in the picture? Do you think the person/animal is happy or sad? Why?* Have more advanced students write their predictions on photocopies of the Sneak a Peek sheet. After reviewing and discussing all the book's illustrations, read the story aloud. Compare the predictions to the actual story. Discuss with students the benefits of looking at story illustrations before reading the corresponding text. Repeat the activity using other picture books.

Variation: Cover the illustrations and read aloud the corresponding text. Discuss as a class what should be included in the pictures. Uncover the illustrations and compare the suggestions to the actual pictures.

Read a Picture

Materials

- nonfiction picture books
- chalkboard and chalk

Reading Strategies

▶ Using **prior knowledge** to add meaning to text

▶ Looking at **picture clues** to predict story content

Write on the chalkboard two or three vocabulary words from a nonfiction story. Select words that directly connect to illustrations in the book. Show students each page of the book and have them use picture clues to predict information included in the story. Ask "how" and "why" questions to help students examine the pictures carefully. Read aloud and define the words on the chalkboard. Invite students to use the listed words to describe the book illustrations. Have students identify which words best describe each picture. After matching vocabulary words to book illustrations, read the story aloud. Have students compare their predictions to the facts in the story.

Match 'em Up

Materials

- student reading books
- transparencies
- paper clips
- wipe-off markers

Reading Strategies

▶ Using **prior knowledge** to add meaning to text

▶ Looking at **picture clues** to predict story content

▶ Using **letter sounds** to pronounce and identify unfamiliar words

Have students turn to a page in their book that includes an illustration clearly described in the text. Ask students to paper-clip a transparency on top of the page. Have the class use wipe-off markers to draw circles around illustrated objects you identify aloud. (Choose objects specifically mentioned in the text.) After students have circled each object, ask them to look for and draw a box around the corresponding word in the passage. Guide students by pointing out phonetic clues and letter combinations that can be used to locate the word, such as the /ou/ sound in *house.* Have students draw a line from the boxed word to the circled object to emphasize that picture clues can help the reader identify words in text. Repeat the activity using other book pages.

Goldilocks went into the three bears' house.

 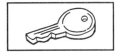 

Stick 'em Up

Materials

- large picture book with predictable text
- large stick-on notes
- black marker

Reading Strategies

▶ Using **prior knowledge** to add meaning to text

▶ Looking at **picture clues** to determine story content

▶ Using **letter sounds** to pronounce and identify unfamiliar words

In advance, look through a large picture book and find words in the text that correspond to the illustrations. Write the words on separate large stick-on notes and stick them on the chalkboard. Discuss with students the illustrations in the book and then read the story together. Read aloud the words on the chalkboard and invite students to stick each note to the corresponding illustrated object. Help students read the words and find the best choice by asking questions about letter sounds. For example, *What letter sound do you hear at the beginning of the word? Is there another clue in the middle or at the end of the word that might help you identify the answer?*

Variation: Teach "Stick 'em Up" as a picture-matching game. Make two identical sets of photocopied, laminated picture and word cards. Tape small, flat magnets to the backs of the cards, and attach each set to the opposite ends of the chalkboard (or other magnetic surface). Divide the class into two teams and have team members take turns matching words with pictures. The first team to correctly match all the pictures and words wins.

On the Road to Reading

Materials

- chalkboard (or other magnetic surface)

  laminated construction-paper car

- a small, thin magnet

- tape

- picture book

Reading Strategies

▶ Using **prior knowledge** to add meaning to text

▶ Looking at **picture clues** to predict story content

In advance, draw a winding road on the chalkboard. Tape a small, flat magnet to the back of a laminated construction-paper car and place the car at the beginning of the road. Have students preview a picture book, looking at the illustrations to find clues about the story. Ask the class to predict what happens at the beginning of the story and then write their suggestions on the road, just ahead of the car. Invite a volunteer to move the magnetic car slightly up the road. Have students help you decide what to write for the next part of the story. Continue moving the car and writing predictions until the entire story sequence is written on the road. Read the story aloud and have students compare their predictions to the actual story.

Lightning Flash

Materials

- nonfiction animal picture book
- chalkboard and chalk
- tape

Reading Strategies

▶ Using **prior knowledge** to add meaning to text

▶ Using **prior knowledge** to develop background information

Draw on the chalkboard a picture of a cloud surrounded by four or five lightning bolts. Tape in the center of the cloud a picture of an animal. Write on different lightning bolts category headings, such as *What It Looks Like, What It Eats, Where It Lives,* and *What It Can Do.* Have students identify the picture and share aloud what they know about the animal. Ask them to give one- or two-word facts about the animal as you write their ideas under the appropriate category on the chalkboard. Set a time limit (one minute) to encourage students to think quickly. Read a corresponding nonfiction animal story aloud and compare facts written on the chalkboard to those given in the book. Discuss together the benefits of thinking about a topic before reading about it in a book.

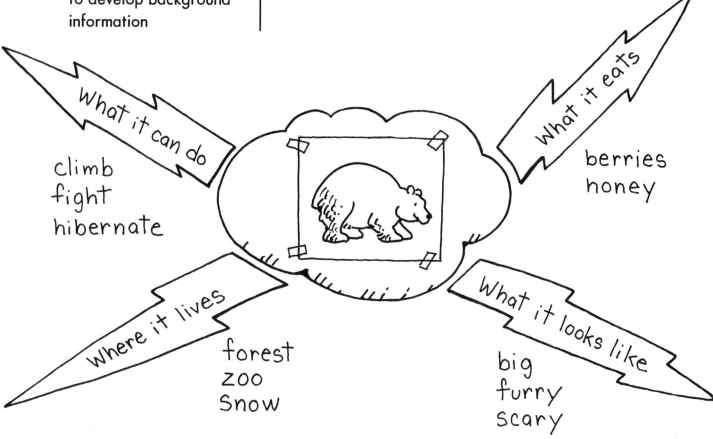

Read A Rhyme

Materials

- Read a Rhyme sheets (pages 88–89)
- overhead transparency and projector (optional)
- nursery rhymes

Reading Strategies

▶ Using **prior knowledge** to add meaning to text

▶ Listening for **context clues** to identify unfamiliar words

▶ Comparing similar **letter patterns** to identify rhyming words

Read aloud the rhymes from the Read a Rhyme sheet. (If you wish, show the rhymes on an overhead projector to increase students' print awareness.) Invite students to listen to the rhymes and identify the missing words. Point out different reading strategies that can be used, such as listening for and matching repetitive letter patterns, recognizing descriptive words that help identify the missing word, and relying on prior knowledge to select words that make sense in the text. Repeat this activity using additional rhyming poems and songs. Choose text unfamiliar to students so they rely on reading strategies rather than using recall to identify missing words.

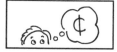 

Get On with It

Materials

- nonfiction picture book
- chalkboard and chalk

Reading Strategies

▶ Using **prior knowledge** to add meaning to text

▶ Using **picture clues** to predict story content

Identify for students the topic or theme of a nonfiction book and then write the heading *Old Information* on the chalkboard. Invite students to brainstorm facts they know about the topic as you write their ideas under the heading. (Write all facts given, even if they are incorrect.) Preview together the pictures in the book and then read the story aloud. Invite students to share new facts they've learned from the book. Write their ideas on the chalkboard under the heading *New Information*. Have students compare old and new facts to help them see the relationship between prior knowledge and new learning. Highlight on the chalkboard the facts students "knew ahead of time" and cross out the information that was inaccurate. Discuss how "old" information helps readers predict and understand words in print.

Old Information

Bears are furry.
Bears eat honey.
Bears live in forests and zoos.
Bears can climb trees.

New Information

There are seven kinds of bears.
They don't see or hear well.
They have sharp teeth and claws.

Use It and Lose It

Materials

- student reading materials
- chalkboard and chalk

Reading Strategies

▶ Using **prior knowledge** to add meaning to text

▶ Listening for **context clues** to identify unfamiliar words

In advance, write on the chalkboard three or four challenging vocabulary words from student reading materials. Ask students to guess what the words mean as you write their ideas on the chalkboard. Read the picture book or textbook passage aloud and have students listen to how the vocabulary words are being used. Invite students to revise their definitions based on what they hear. Write these new definitions alongside the others on the chalkboard. Define the words for students and have them compare your definitions to those written on the board. Have students rephrase your definitions to check whether they clearly understand the meaning of each word. Challenge the class to correctly use each vocabulary word three different times throughout the day. Make a game of it by keeping a tally and inviting volunteers to erase the word off the chalkboard after it has been successfully used three times.

Huh?

Materials

- student reading materials
- writing paper

Reading Strategies

▶ Using **prior knowledge** to determine if sentences make sense

▶ Using rules of **grammar** to identify reading errors

▶ Using **context clues** to identify reading errors

In advance, rewrite a textbook passage so it contains several errors that affect the meaning of the text, for example unfamiliar words or improper word usage. Discuss with students the importance of "reading for meaning." Tell students they need to understand what they are reading and not just say the words. Read the modified passage aloud without pausing or interrupting the flow of words. When you are finished, ask students questions about the passage. Discuss how the mistakes make it difficult to answer the questions. Reread the passage, this time asking students to say *Huh?* out loud each time they hear you read something that does not make sense. Help students look for context clues that clarify what is being read. Emphasize the importance of "listening" to sentences and taking time to look for answers when the meaning is unclear.

Variation: Invite more advanced learners to read along as you reread the text aloud. Have students cover the text page with a transparency and use erasable crayons to circle parts of the passage that are confusing.

 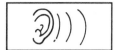
Stomp It Out

Materials

- picture book
- writing paper
- chalkboard and chalk

Reading Strategies

▶ Using **letter sounds** to identify and pronounce words

▶ Using **prior knowledge** to add meaning to text

In advance, copy on paper three- and four-letter words from a picture book. (Choose words that begin and end with a consonant.) Read the story aloud and discuss with students any challenging vocabulary words. Write the selected three- and four-letter words on the chalkboard, omitting the vowels. Tell students that the words on the chalkboard are from the story. Invite the class to determine the identity of each word by having students sound out beginning and ending word parts while marching in place. Ask them to step on their right foot as they say the beginning sound, and then have them step on their left foot as they say the ending sound. Encourage students to march faster and faster as they blend the sounds together. Invite students to shout out the word when they know it. After students guess each word, fill in the missing vowels and read the word together.

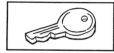 

Poppers

Materials

- overhead transparency and projector
- wipe-off marker

Reading Strategies

▶ Using **context clues** to identify missing words

▶ Using beginning **letter sounds** to identify missing words

In advance, write on an overhead transparency a list of sentences, each of which contains a "clue word" that describes a key word (i.e., a noun, adjective, or verb). Erase the ending letters of each key word and underline the corresponding clue word, for example, *The little girl was so sad she began to c____.* Display the sentences on an overhead projector. Use the sentences to introduce and discuss "poppers" to students. Explain to the class that when they come across a word they don't recognize in a story, they should look for clue words and try a "popper"—say the beginning sound and see what word "pops" in their head. Oftentimes the guessed word is correct; auditory clues in combination with context clues help the reader identify unfamiliar words. Read the sentence aloud and invite students to use "poppers" to help identify the missing words. Have students "fill in the blanks" and recite the sentences to see if the chosen words make sense.

The g——— hit the ball with a b———.

Pop It Out

Materials

● chalkboard and chalk

Reading Strategies

▶ Using **context clues** to identify missing words

▶ Using beginning **letter sounds** to complete sentences

In advance, write a list of sentences that support the use of "poppers" (see page 35). Divide the class into teams and have them line up single file, facing the front of the class. Read one of the sentences aloud, saying just the initial sound for the deleted word. Ask the first person in each line to identify the missing word. The student who says the missing word first earns a point for his or her team. Ask both students to go to the end of the line as you continue the game with the new leaders. End the game when all the sentences have been read and each student has had at least one turn. The team with the most points wins.

Extension: Have players guess the missing word and then use the word in another sentence. This gives students more practice applying their understanding of context clues and word associations.

 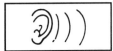

Stop and Say

Materials

- craft sticks
- markers
- multiple copies of a reading book

Reading Strategies

▶ Using **context clues** to predict and identify words

▶ Using **letter sounds** to pronounce and identify words

Invite each student to color a craft stick to make a personalized "reading stick." Distribute reading books and have students use their reading sticks to follow along as you read the text aloud. Ask them to move their reading sticks under the words they hear you say. Pause before each key word in a sentence and have students read the word aloud. Choose words at the ends of sentences to provide more context clues for students to use as they "fill in the blanks." Also choose nouns or words used to describe story illustrations—these words are easier for students to identify. For more advanced learning, choose random words for the class to identify and read.

Variations: To help students see similarities among words, pause before the words that fit a particular letter pattern, such as rhyming words. Or, invite partners to complete this activity independently, having one student in each pair read aloud while the other follows along and "fills in the blanks."

Give It Meaning

Materials

- student reading materials
- sentence strips
- pocket chart
- index cards

Reading Strategies

▶ Using **context clues** to identify unfamiliar words

▶ Using **prior knowledge** to determine if sentences make sense

In advance, copy on sentence strips a paragraph from student reading materials. Place the sentence strips in proper sequence in a pocket chart. Write some nonsense words on index cards and place each card in the pocket chart over a key word in a sentence. Read the sentences aloud (or invite volunteers to read them) and invite students to use context clues to help them "translate" the nonsense words (i.e., guess the hidden words). Encourage students to listen to (or look at) the entire sentence before making their predictions. Emphasize the importance of looking for clues in the text rather than trying to read the nonsense words. Explain that being able to pronounce words may not always help understand what they mean. Invite volunteers to remove the cards after they think they know what the hidden words are. After all nonsense words are removed, read the "translated" passage together.

Hide and Seek

Materials

- student reading materials
- overhead transparency and projector
- masking tape

Reading Strategies

▶ Using **context clues** to identify missing words

▶ Using **prior knowledge** to add meaning to text

Make an overhead transparency of a passage from student reading materials. Cover some words in the text with masking tape. Choose nouns at the ends of sentences; these words are the easiest for children to identify. Discuss how sentences often contain "clue words" that help us determine the meaning of other words in the text. Place the transparency on an overhead projector and then read aloud (or ask volunteers to read) each sentence, saying *blank* for each deleted word. Have students guess the identity of the hidden words. Invite volunteers to remove the masking tape to see if the predictions were correct.

Extension: For a greater challenge, cover words at the beginning and in the middle of the sentences rather than at the end. Cover critical adjectives and verbs as well as nouns.

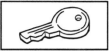 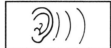

It's Your Choice

Materials

- chalkboard and chalk

Reading Strategies

▶ Using **context clues** to identify missing words

▶ Using rules of **grammar** to help select appropriate words

Write on the chalkboard simple sentences pertaining to a recent unit of study. Delete a verb or a noun from each sentence, leaving the rest of the words to serve as context clues. After each sentence, write three words as possible replacements—a first word that is the opposite part of speech; a second word that is the correct part of speech, but does not fit the sentence semantically (it makes no sense); and a third word that correctly completes the sentence. Invite students to choose the word that both sounds right and makes sense in the sentence to "fill in the blank."

Ah Ha!

Materials

- challenging vocabulary words
- index cards
- sentence strips
- pocket chart

Reading Strategies

▶ Using **context clues** to identify unfamiliar words

▶ Using **prior knowledge** to add meaning to text

In advance, write vocabulary words on separate index cards and write sentences containing those words on separate sentence strips. (Be certain the sentences also contain context clues to help identify the vocabulary words.) Place each card faceup in the pocket chart, followed by the corresponding sentence strip placed facedown. Read aloud the first vocabulary word and have students predict its meaning. Invite a volunteer to turn over the corresponding sentence strip. Have the class read the sentence aloud. Ask students to revise their definition based on how the word is used in the sentence. Discuss how reading a word within the context of a sentence can help define it. Have the class continue defining and redefining the remaining vocabulary words. For an extra challenge, invite students to think of new sentences that contain the vocabulary words. Have them write their own vocabulary cards and sentences to share with the class.

Variation: Include picture clues to go with the vocabulary cards. First show the word and then a matching picture before turning over the corresponding sentence strip.

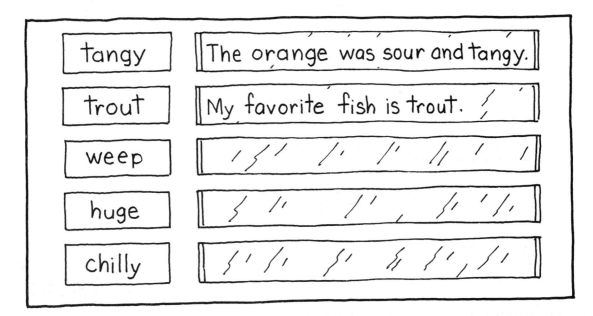

tangy	The orange was sour and tangy.
trout	My favorite fish is trout.
weep	
huge	
chilly	

Look Before You Leap

Materials

- Look Before You Leap sheet (page 90)

- student reading materials

- scissors

- crayons or markers

- craft sticks

- tape

Reading Strategies

▶ Using **context clues** to identify missing words

▶ Using **prior knowledge** to add meaning to text

In advance, photocopy the Look Before You Leap sheet and cut apart the frog pictures. Give each student a frog cutout to color and tape to a craft stick. Discuss why it is important for students to "read on" when they encounter an unfamiliar word in a story. Explain that unfamiliar words can often be identified by continuing to read and looking for clue words. Invite students to use their frog sticks to point to each word as they read text aloud. When students encounter an unfamiliar word, have them use their paper frogs to "leap" over the word and continue to read. Invite volunteers to find context clues in the remaining sentences to help them identify the unfamiliar word.

Flip-Up Families

Materials

- Word Families sheets (pages 91–93)
- sentence strips
- paper squares
- marker
- stapler

Reading Strategies

▶ Using **context clues** to identify words that make sense

▶ Using **prior knowledge** to determine if sentences make sense

▶ Looking at **letter patterns** to identify similar words

In advance, select words from the Word Families sheets to include in sentences you write on sentence strips, for example, *I saw a **rat** sit on a **log**.* Write letters (or letter blends) on separate paper squares and staple a stack of these "replacement letters" over beginning consonants of key words in the sentences. Read each sentence strip aloud. Flip up a paper square and show students how the sentence changes, for example, *I saw a **cat** sit on a **dog**.* Flip up the remaining paper squares, one at a time, and invite students to read the new words and sentences. Have students identify which replacement words make sense in the sentences.

Variations: Draw picture clues to help beginning readers identify the new words. Invite more advanced learners to make their own flip-up sentence strips to share with classmates.

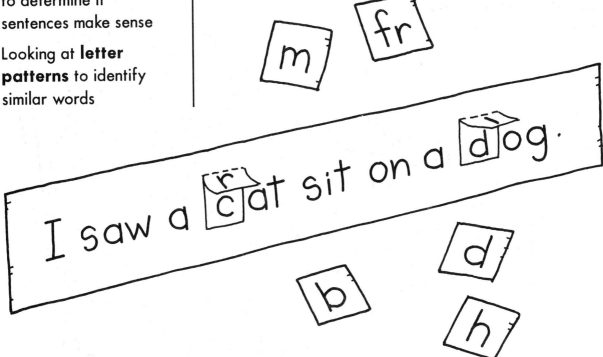

Mix and Match

Materials

- Mix and Match sheet (page 94)
- overhead transparency and projector
- marker
- scissors
- writing paper

Reading Strategies

▶ Using **letter sounds** to pronounce and identify words

▶ Looking at **letter patterns** to identify similar words

In advance, make photocopies and a transparency of the Mix and Match sheet. Cut apart the transparency vowels and use an overhead projector to show students how to place the squares between various consonant pairs to form a variety of words. Demonstrate how changing the vowels can form additional words, such as *hat, hit, hot,* and *hut.* Divide the class into pairs and give partners a Mix and Match sheet. Have one student from each pair cut apart and move the vowel squares between different consonants on the page while partners write a list of the words formed. Ask students to read their word lists aloud, decide together which ones are nonsense words, and cross the nonsense words off the list. Compare the words formed and have the class identify those with similar letter patterns.

Extension: Write alphabet letters on Unifix cubes and invite students to build words. Have them mix and match vowels to form words with similar letter patterns, such as *cat* and *cut.*

Pick and Choose

Materials

● none

Reading Strategies

▶ Listening to **letter sounds** to identify and pronounce words

Invite two students to help you spell out a word to the rest of the class. Whisper a different consonant sound to each volunteer and have him or her say aloud the corresponding letter name. Tell the class a vowel sound to add to the letters to form a word. For example, *Add the* /i/ *sound to letters* b *and* g *to make a word.* The first student who identifies the word chooses a vowel sound for the next word. He or she also chooses two new volunteers to help select new consonants. Repeat the process, having volunteers say aloud consonant names and asking the winner from the last round to think of and say aloud a vowel sound.

Variation: Include visual cues by writing the chosen consonants (not the vowel sound) on the chalkboard after volunteers say them aloud or by having volunteers hold up corresponding alphabet cards.

Blending Race

Materials

- picture book
- chalkboard and chalk
- writing paper (optional)

Reading Strategies

▶ Listening to **letter sounds** and identifying corresponding alphabet letters

▶ Looking at **letter patterns** to identify words

In advance, select a list of words from a story recently read aloud. Divide the class into two or three teams and invite one member from each team to the chalkboard. Secretly select a word from the list and then sound out each letter of the word, one letter at a time. Have the players write the corresponding letters on the board as you say the sounds. (You may choose to have other team members silently play along at their desks by having them write the letters on paper.) The first player to identify the word and shout it out loud earns a point for his or her team. Continue playing with different players and words.

Variation: Have students listen as you sound out the entire word. Then have players silently write the word on the board before identifying it aloud.

Word Staircase

Materials

- picture book
- chalkboard and chalk

Reading Strategies

▶ Using **letter sounds** to identify and pronounce words

▶ Looking at **letter patterns** to identify similar words

Read a book aloud. Choose a three- or four-letter word from the story and write it on the chalkboard. (Be sure to choose a word ending in a consonant.) Have students read the word aloud and identify the ending sound. Ask them to say a word that begins with that same sound. Write the word vertically on the chalkboard, beginning it with the last letter of the word already written on the board. For example, write the word *rat* downward from the letter *r* in the word *bear*. Have students think of another word, one that begins with the last letter of the second word (e.g., *t* in *rat*). Write the third word horizontally, beginning it with the last letter from the second word. Continue this process to make a "staircase" of connected words on the chalkboard. For an extra challenge, ask students to think of words related to a theme, such as animal names.

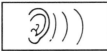

I Spy

Materials

- I Spy sheet (page 95)
- crayons
- overhead transparency and projector
- colored markers
- student reading materials

Reading Strategies

▶ Looking at **letter patterns** to identify similar word parts

▶ Using **letter sounds** to pronounce and identify word parts

Give each student a photocopy of the I Spy sheet. Make an overhead transparency of the sheet to guide students as they complete their work. Say the sound (not the letter names) of different letter combinations (e.g., *en*, *it*, *op*), one at a time, and have students find and circle the corresponding letter patterns in the words on their paper. Have students use a different-colored crayon for each letter pattern, such as a green for *en*, red for *it*, and blue for *op*. Use the transparency and colored markers to guide students as they complete their work. For extra fun, challenge students to "spy" all the requested letter patterns within a set amount of time. Repeat the activity using words from student reading materials.

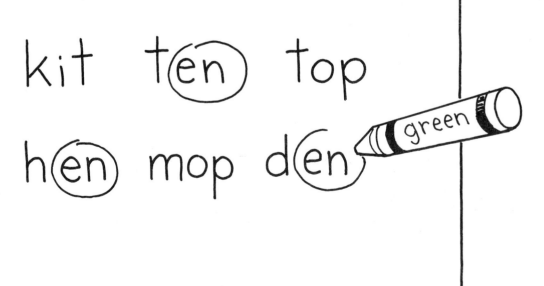

Emergent Readers

Leading Letter

Materials

- student reading materials
- writing paper and pencil
- chalkboard and chalk

Reading Strategies

▶ Using **letter sounds** to pronounce and identify incomplete words

▶ Looking at **letter patterns** to form similar words

Use a pencil to write a list of words from student reading materials, and then erase the first letter in each word. Give each student a photocopy of the list. Demonstrate on the chalk-board how to make complete words by adding initial consonants to word endings on the list. For example, add the letter *c* to *-at* to form the word *cat*. Sound out the word parts so students hear as well as see the formation of the word. Discuss and demonstrate how to use other consonants to form additional words, such as *hat, bat,* and *mat.* Have students work independently or with partners to complete the list of words. Invite students to read aloud the words they have spelled.

Word-Family Strips

Materials

- 1½" x 10" (3.8 cm x 25 cm) construction-paper strips

- black marker

- index cards

- tape

- Word Families sheets (pages 91–93)

- writing paper (optional)

Reading Strategies

▶ Using **letter sounds** to pronounce similar words

▶ Looking at **letter patterns** to identify similar words

▶ Using **prior knowledge** to identify "sense" and "nonsense" words

In advance, make a variety of "letter strips" by writing letters or letter blends down the length of paper strips. Make a sliding cover for each strip by folding an index card around the width of the strip and taping the ends together. Cut a "window" in the front of each cover and write a letter cluster to the right of the window so that when the strip is pulled, new words are formed. For example, pull an alphabet strip through a cover with *an* written to the right of the window to form words such as *can, fan, man,* and *pan.* (See pages 91–93 for a selection of letter clusters to choose from.) Emphasize to students that not all letter combinations make real words—some make "nonsense words," such as *gan* and *lan.* Divide the class into pairs, and invite partners to form words using the word-family strips. Have students say aloud or copy on paper the newly formed words.

House of Words

Materials

- chalkboard and chalk
- Word Families sheets (pages 91–93)
- blank books

Reading Strategies

▶ Listening to **letter sounds** and identifying corresponding alphabet letters

▶ Using **letter patterns** to form similar words

Draw a simple outline of a house on the chalkboard. Choose a letter pattern from the Word Families sheets and write the pattern on the roof of the house. Explain to students that to "live" in the house, words must contain the letter pattern written on the roof. Have students brainstorm words that contain the pattern as you write their responses inside the house outline. For example, if the letter pattern is *-ake,* the words *bake, rake, snake,* and *lake* are correct responses. Give each student a blank book and invite him or her to copy the house outline and the words in the book. When they are finished, invite students to read aloud the words they have written. Each week, have students add a new "house of words" to their books.

Colorful Words

Materials

- Colorful Words sheets (pages 96–98)

  scissors

- glue

- index cards

- crayons or markers

- student reading materials

Reading Strategies

▶ Looking at **letter patterns** to identify words within words

▶ Using **letter sounds** to identify and pronounce words within words

In advance, use the Colorful Words sheets to make color-coded word cards. First, cut out the words and paste them onto separate index cards. Then, color the smaller word within each word (e.g., *top* in *stop*) one color and the rest of the letters black. Show the flash cards to the class, one card at a time, and have students read the color-coded words only. Show the cards again, this time having students read the entire text after they read the color-coded word (e.g., *top…stop*). For extra fun, try a "lightning" round in which the class reads the words in rapid sequence. This encourages students to automatically see the "part" as it fits into the "whole." Make more color-coded cards each week by using words from student reading materials. Invite students to use the flash cards with partners or in small groups.

Rainbow Clues

Materials

- chalkboard and colored chalk

Reading Strategies

▶ Highlighting **letter patterns** to see similar word parts

▶ Looking at **letter patterns** to identify words within words

Start each school day by writing on the chalkboard a question about a fun fact. For example, *What animal sleeps while hanging upside down?* Rather than reading the question aloud, use colored chalk to highlight various letter patterns, or "chunks" within the words, one pattern at a time. For example, underline word endings (e.g., *–ing* in *hanging*), put a box around "hidden" words (e.g., *up* in *upside*), and draw brackets around "2-fers" (two letters that make one sound, such as *ow* in *down*). This will help students see the contextual and structural clues that can help them read the text. After everything is marked in the text, read the question together. Discuss how looking for letter patterns helps a reader decode words. Finish the activity by inviting students to guess the answer to the question.

Extension: Ask students to copy the question off the board (or give them photocopies), and have them use colored pencils to highlight the letter patterns.

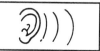 
Build a Word

Materials

- Alphabet Cards (pages 99–101)

- scissors

- plastic resealable bags

Reading Strategies

▶ Listening to **letter sounds** and identifying corresponding letters of the alphabet

▶ Using **letter patterns** to identify and spell similar words

Give each student a photocopy of the Alphabet Cards to cut apart and store in plastic resealable bags. Ask students to use their cards to spell out and identify a "secret" word. Have them listen as you say each letter-sound of the word (in proper sequence), and then ask them to find the corresponding paper letter. Have students arrange the letters in the order they are heard. After students have identified the secret word, have them form new words by rearranging or subtracting letters already on display. Invite more advanced students to add additional letters to form other words, such as adding *er* to the word *box* to form *boxer*. Repeat with new words and letters. For an extra challenge, call out letters in random order and have students rearrange letters to identify the word.

 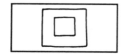 

Scavenger Hunt

Materials

- Scavenger Hunt sheet (page 102)

- chalkboard and chalk

- crayons

Reading Strategies

▶ Highlighting **letter patterns** to see words within words

▶ Using **letter sounds** to identify words within words

Make a photocopy of the Scavenger Hunt sheet for each student. Explain how little words can be used to recognize and pronounce big words. Write the word *pit* on the chalkboard and cover the letter *p* to show the "hidden" word *it.* Have students say the words *it* and *pit* aloud to hear as well as see the hidden word. Emphasize the importance of both seeing and "hearing" the word. Discuss how some letter combinations may look like hidden words, but they are pronounced differently (e.g., *it* in *kite*). Give each student a Scavenger Hunt sheet and have him or her use crayons to draw a box around each hidden word. (Note that Hunt 1 contains only hidden words *at, is, it, an, in,* and *as.*) Invite students to identify each hidden word and then read the corresponding big word.

  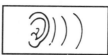

Fixer-Upper

Materials

- student reading materials
- tape recorder and cassette tape
- overhead transparency and projector
- markers
- writing paper

Reading Strategies

▶ Using rules of **grammar** to identify errors in sentence structure

▶ Using **prior knowledge** to determine if sentences make sense

▶ Listening to **letter sounds** to identify mispronounced words

In advance, rewrite a paragraph from student reading materials so that it contains several grammatical errors. Make both a transparency copy and a tape recording of this revised passage. Explain to students that when a sentence contains mistakes and is read incorrectly, it doesn't "sound right." Have students listen to the tape recording, and ask them to keep a tally of how many mistakes they hear in the story. After students have listened to the tape, place the transparency on an overhead projector and read the sentences aloud. Invite volunteers to circle the grammatical errors on the transparency. Count the number of errors in the passage, and then have students compare that amount to the number of mistakes they heard on the tape. Rewrite the sentences correctly and invite students to read the revised paragraph aloud.

Variation: Make photocopies of the transparency and have more advanced learners work independently to find and circle the mistakes in the passage.

 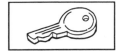 
Letter Snatcher

Materials

- Letter Snatcher sheet (page 103)
- overhead transparency and projector
- marker

Reading Strategies

▶ Looking at **letter patterns** to identify missing letters in words

▶ Using **letter sounds** to identify and pronounce incomplete words

▶ Using **context clues** to identify incomplete words in a sentence

▶ Using **prior knowledge** to determine if words make sense in a sentence

In advance, make an overhead transparency of the Letter Snatcher sheet. Use an overhead projector to show students the sentences. Explain that a "Letter Snatcher" has stolen letters in the words. Have the students read the passage "as is"—the story context will help them "fill in the gaps." Guide students by having them sound out letters, look at letter patterns, and search for context clues in the sentences. Write vowels *a, e, i, o,* and *u* at the top of the page as a visual prompt. If students are still having difficulty, draw illustrations (picture clues) to match each paragraph's theme. Invite the class to determine which missing letters belong in each word. Write their answers on the transparency and read together the completed sentences.

Extension: Make additional Letter Snatcher sheets using text from student reading materials. Invite students to make their own "fill in the blank" worksheets for classmates to complete.

We h_ve a p_t c_t. Her n_me is Fl_ffy.

 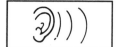

Sticky Words

Materials

- index cards
- overhead transparency and projector
- marker
- tape

Reading Strategies

▶ Using **prior knowledge** to determine whether sentences make sense

▶ Using rules of **grammar** to read sentences correctly

In advance, write the words of simple sentences on separate index cards. Copy the sentences onto a transparency, but omit at least one verb, pronoun, or conjunction in each sentence. Place the transparency on an overhead projector and read the first sentence aloud. Ask students if the sentence sounds right—if it makes sense. Identify the missing word(s) and explain that when words are omitted or used incorrectly in sentences, the meaning is unclear. Discuss how some words (e.g., conjunctions, verbs) act as "sticky words" and connect parts of a sentence together to make the meaning clearer. Divide the class into partners and give each pair a strip of tape and the word cards needed to form a complete sentence. Ask students to tape the word cards together in proper sequence. Read together the remaining incomplete sentences displayed on the overhead and invite partners to share their taped sentences to identify the missing "sticky words."

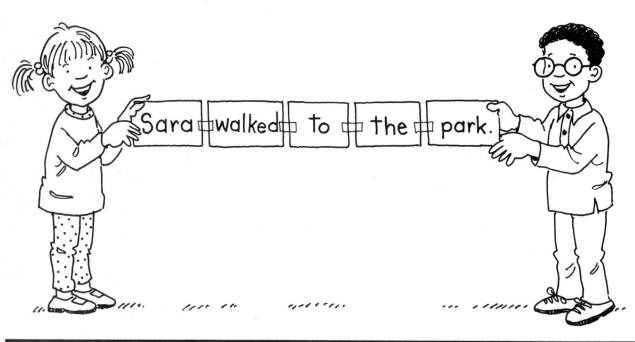

The Attribute Game

Materials

- The Attribute Game sheet (page 104)
- chalkboard and chalk

Reading Strategies

▶ Listening to **letter sounds** to identifying corresponding alphabet letters

▶ Using **prior knowledge** to decide if words make sense

▶ Using rules of **grammar** to spell words correctly

In advance, draw one of the grids from the Attribute Game sheet on the chalkboard. Discusss how looking for clues in text can help a reader identify unfamiliar words. Explain to students that they are to use clues in the grid to identify "mystery words." Model how to use and fill in the grid by "intersecting" a vertical and horizontal clue to help identify each mystery noun (for example, *red* and *eat* both describe the noun *apple*). Invite children to complete the activity orally as you write their responses on the grid, or invite partners to fill in photocopies of the Attribute Game sheet. (Note: You may wish to provide a list of nouns for children to choose from.)

Extension: Make additional attribute grids using words from student reading materials. Invite students to make their own attribute grids for classmates to complete.

	red	green	blue
food	apple	gra	
outside	stop sign		
animal	ladybug		

Red-Flag It

Materials

- student reading material

- writing paper

- red construction-paper flags

Reading Strategies

▶ Using **prior knowledge** to determine if sentences make sense

▶ Using rules of **grammar** to identify errors

▶ Listening to **letter sounds** to identify mispronounced words

▶ Using **context clues** to identify misused words

In advance, rewrite student text so that it contains grammatical mistakes and misused words. Discuss with students the importance of "reading for meaning." Explain that when a person reads a sentence that makes no sense, the confusion should serve as a "red flag"—an indication that something is grammatically wrong. The person should then reread the sentence and correct it. Distribute a red flag to each student. Have the class listen to you read the rewritten passage. Ask students to hold up the red flag every time they hear a phrase or sentence they do not understand. After reading the entire text without stopping, go back to the beginning and discuss each "red flag" situation with students.

Extension: After reading the passage aloud, give students photocopies of the altered text and have them draw red flags around words or phrases to highlight the problem areas. Invite students to share and discuss their answers.

The Missing Link

Materials

- student reading materials
- chalkboard and chalk

Reading Strategies

▶ Using **context clues** to identify unfamiliar words

▶ Using **prior knowledge** to determine if sentences make sense

Write on the chalkboard several sentences containing context clues for challenging vocabulary words, for example, *The gigantic bear was as big as a house.* Circle the word you want students to define. Read the first sentence aloud and ask students to define the circled word. Offer some incorrect answers, such as *little* for the word *gigantic.* Explain to students that sentences often contain clue words or "missing links" that can help readers define unfamiliar words. Circle the clue word in the first sentence and then show students how to draw a line to "link" the two circles together. Discuss the importance of using context clues to determine if definitions for unfamiliar words "make sense" and "fit" the rest of the story. Continue with the remaining sentences, inviting volunteers to circle and connect word pairs.

The (gigantic) bear was as (large) as a house.

Word Translator

Materials

- Word Translator sheet (page 105)
- overhead transparency and projector
- marker

Reading Strategies

▶ Using **context clues** to identify missing words

▶ Using **prior knowledge** to add meaning to text

In advance, write a list of six sentences, each one containing a nonsense word along with context clues to help identify the word. Underline the nonsense word in each sentence, for example, *It was raining so she put up her isumla.* Make a transparency of the sentences along with the Word Translator sheet. Also make photocopies of both sheets for students. Discuss with the class how reading ahead in a sentence and looking for context clues can often help the reader "translate" unfamiliar words. Distribute the photocopies to students. Ask the class to identify the meaning of nonsense words using context clues in the sentences. Have students write on the Word Translator sheet each nonsense word at one end of a "translator" and then write the word translation at the other end. Use the transparencies to guide students as they work. Invite students to share and discuss their answers. For extra fun, invite students to write their own nonsense sentences for classmates to "translate."

Word Associations

Materials

- chalkboard and chalk
- writing paper

Reading Strategies

▶ Using **prior knowledge** to brainstorm theme-related words and sentences

▶ Comparing **letter sounds** to form similar words

Write a theme-related word vertically on the chalkboard. Invite students to use each letter in the word to form other words related to the same theme. For example, students may think of the words *water, humpback, animal, lungs,* and *eat* for the letters in the word ***whale.*** Write the new words horizontally on the chalkboard so that students will use the letters in the original word. Brainstorm with students a sentence for each new word and write the sentences on the chalkboard, adding the words next to the ones already written. Invite students to read the sentences aloud, or have them copy the sentences onto paper and draw matching illustrations.

Extension: Repeat the activity with another theme-related word, this time having students work with partners to write the words and sentences.

 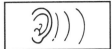

Telephone Spelling

Materials

- Telephone Spelling sheet (page 106)
- class spelling or vocabulary list
- writing paper

Reading Strategies

▶ Using **letter sounds** to pronounce and identify words

▶ Using **prior knowledge** to add meaning to text

Prepare a list of "coded" spelling or vocabulary words by referring to buttons on a telephone and replacing letters with numbers, for example, 7-4-2-7-5 for the word *shark*. Make photocopies of the list along with the Telephone Spelling sheet. Have students use the telephone illustration to "translate" and then match the number codes to corresponding words on their spelling or vocabulary list. (Note: There may be more than one translation for each number code. For example, 7-4-2-7-5 could spell *ricrl*. Tell students to select the "translation" that makes sense and matches a word on their spelling or vocabulary list.) Have students write the translated words at the bottom of the Telephone Spelling sheet.

Variation: Have students use Telephone Spelling sheets to calculate the "value" of words from their spelling or vocabulary lists, for example, *shark* is worth a value of $7 + 4 + 2 + 7 + 5 = 25$. Invite students to predict and then calculate the word with the highest value. For extra fun, invite students to use play phones and punch in words for their partners to guess.

Grab-Bag Game

Materials

- student reading materials
- paper strips
- lunch bag
- chalkboard and chalk

Reading Strategies

▶ Listening to **letter sounds** to identify "secret" words

▶ Using **prior knowledge** to identify "secret" words

Write on separate paper strips key vocabulary words and their synonyms. Fold the strips in half and place them inside a "grab bag." Demonstrate how to secretly select a word from the bag and give clues to the word's identity. For example, you might say *I'm thinking of a word that means "pretty" and it begins with the sound /b/.* Then invite students to select words from the grab bag and take turns giving clues to the class. Have the first student who correctly guesses the word write the answer on the chalkboard. When everyone has taken his or her turn, have the class read through the list of words written on the chalkboard.

Variation: Give students a list of the secret words and synonyms to refer to as classmates give clues. Have students circle their answers before sharing them aloud.

Try-ers

Materials

- Try-ers sheet (page 107)
- chart paper

Reading Strategies

▶ Using **context clues** to identify words used incorrectly

▶ Using **letter sounds** to identify and pronounce parts of a word

Explain to students that some letter combinations have two correct pronunciations, such as /ow/ in *low* and /ow/ in *clown*. Tell them that these types of combinations are called "try-ers" because the only way to know which pronunciation is correct is by trying each sound and deciding which one makes more sense in the sentence. Distribute photocopies of the Try-ers sheet to students. Read together the different ways to pronounce each letter combination in isolated words. When students are comfortable with the different sounds, read the sentences together and stop before each "try-er." Have students decide, based on context clues, which pronunciation is correct. Throughout the following few weeks, invite students to find other "try-ers" in their reading materials. Keep a list of examples on chart paper for students to use as a reference.

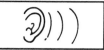 

Word Stretcher

Materials

- Word Families sheets (pages 91–93)
- chalkboard and chalk

Reading Strategies

▶ Using **letter sounds** to form new words

▶ Using **letter patterns** to identify similar words

Copy on the chalkboard a letter pattern from the Word Families sheet. Demonstrate how letters can be substituted or added to the letter pattern to form new words, for example, adding the letter *k* to *-it* to form *kit*. Invite students to brainstorm a list of words that fit the pattern (e.g., *bit*, *sit*, and *fit*). Remind students that their answers must be "real" words, not just random letter combinations. Draw lines to connect each new word to the written letter pattern. Make "branches" from the lines when the new word can be altered to form several additional words, for example, *sit* to *skit*, *slit*, and *spit*. Keep a tally of the number of new words formed. Do a "word stretcher" each week and challenge students to beat the previous week's tally.

Variation: Have students write the words on paper dolls and tape the dolls together to link those with similar letter patterns.

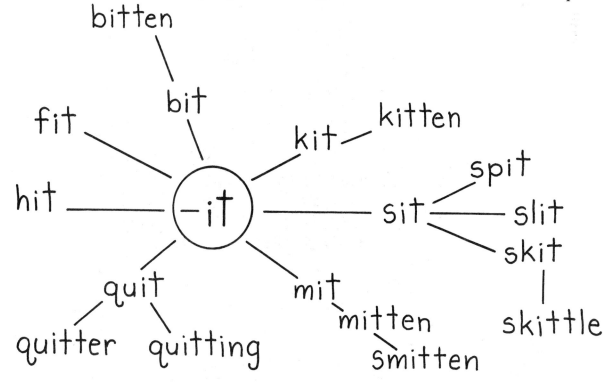

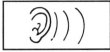

Shift and Change

Materials

- Shift and Change sheet (page 108)

- writing paper (optional)

- Alphabet Cards (pages 99–101)

- Word Families sheets (pages 91–93)

Reading Strategies

▶ Listening to **letter sounds** and identifying corresponding alphabet letters

▶ Using **letter patterns** to spell words correctly

Use the Shift and Change sheet to guide students as they add, omit, or substitute letters in one word to form additional words. Invite students to write the words on paper or have them manipulate alphabet cards. Use words from the Word Families sheets to make additional "scripts" for the students to follow. Increase the difficulty by giving students definitions instead of word prompts. For example, instead of saying *Change one letter in the word* boat *to form the word* coat, say *Change the letter* b *in the word* boat *to describe something you wear when it's cold* (coat).

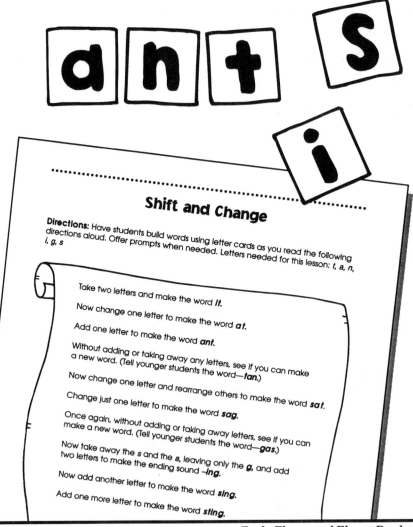

Shift and Change

Directions: Have students build words using letter cards as you read the following directions aloud. Offer prompts when needed. Letters needed for this lesson: *t, a, n, i, g, s*

Take two letters and make the word *it.*

Now change one letter to make the word *at.*

Add one letter to make the word *ant.*

Without adding or taking away any letters, see if you can make a new word. (Tell younger students the word—*tan.*)

Now change one letter and rearrange others to make the word *sat.*

Change just one letter to make the word *sag.*

Once again, without adding or taking away letters, see if you can make a new word. (Tell younger students the word—*gas.*)

Now take away the *s* and the *a*, leaving only the *g*, and add two letters to make the ending sound *–ing.*

Now add another letter to make the word *sing.*

Add one more letter to make the word *sting.*

Super Sleuth

Materials

- class spelling or vocabulary list
- chalkboard and chalk
- writing paper
- calculators (optional)

Reading Strategies

▶ Listening to **letter sounds** and identifying corresponding alphabet letters

▶ Using **letter patterns** to spell words correctly

Write on the chalkboard a multisyllabic word from the class spelling or vocabulary list. Divide the class into partners and give each pair a sheet of paper. Ask students to use the letters of the word to make a list of additional words. Write a few examples on the board. Remind students to look for word families (words that fit the same letter pattern, such as *cake, rake,* and *make*) and words within words. After a designated period of time, have partners stop forming words and calculate the total points earned—one point for each one-letter word, two points for each two-letter word, and so on. Repeat the process using other words from the word list.

 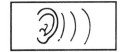 

Guess My Word

Materials

- storybook
- index cards
- paper bag
- chalkboard and chalk

Reading Strategies

▶ Pronouncing and combining **letter sounds** to identify words

▶ Using **prior knowledge** to identify words that make sense

Choose vocabulary words from a recently read story and write them on separate index cards. Fold the cards in half and place them in a paper bag. Invite a volunteer to secretly select a word from the bag. Write the middle letter of the word on the chalkboard, and write blank lines for the remaining letters. Have students try to guess the "mystery" word. Invite the volunteer to fill in one of the blanks that is to the immediate right or left of the letter already written on the board. Continue in this fashion, asking the volunteer to add letters from the middle of the word outward as the class tries to guess the word. Invite the student who correctly identifies the word first to choose the next index card. Repeat the activity with the new mystery word.

Variation: Have the volunteer add letters from left to right. This will give students practice sounding out letters of a word in order rather than looking for letter patterns within words.

Peek-a-Boo Clue

Materials

- overhead transparency and projector
- marker
- construction-paper strips

Reading Strategies

▶ Using **context clues** to identify missing words

▶ Using **prior knowledge** to determine if sentences make sense

In advance, write pairs of sentences on a transparency. The second sentence of each pair should include details about a key word used in the first, for example, *The girl started to cry. She missed her mother and wanted to go home.* For each pair, erase the key word and cover the second sentence with construction paper. Place the transparency on an overhead projector. Have students read aloud the uncovered sentence in the first pair and then guess the identity of the missing word. Remove the construction-paper strip and read the "partner" sentence aloud. Identify the context clue in the partner sentence and write the missing word in the other sentence. Discuss how context clues can be found in a sentence that follows an unfamiliar word. Invite students to follow the same procedure to "fill in the blank" for each of the remaining pairs of sentences.

 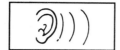

Be the Sentence

Materials

- student reading materials
- sentence strips
- marker
- scissors

Reading Strategies

▶ Using rules of **grammar** to determine the order of words in a sentence

▶ Using **prior knowledge** to determine if sentences make sense

In advance, select several sentences from student reading materials and write the sentences on sentence strips. Cut the strips apart to make word cards. Have groups of students hold up the word cards in proper sequence to rebuild the sentences. Invite each group to stand in front of the class and display the complete sentence. For extra fun, first have students stand with words in scrambled order and then have classmates tell the students how to rearrange themselves so that the sentence makes sense. For an extra challenge, distribute markers and blank sentence-strip pieces and invite student groups to write and build new sentences.

Variation: Complete this activity as a fast-paced game. Give each group of students the same set of sentences and have the teams race to win points building each sentence the quickest.

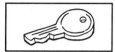 

Skim and Scan

Materials

- student reading materials
- transparencies
- paper clips
- wipe-off markers

Reading Strategies

▶ Using **context clues** to identify missing words

▶ Using **prior knowledge** to add meaning to text

Discuss how "reading on" and glancing through sentences to find key words or phrases helps locate story details. Have students look at a page in their reading materials—one containing at least two paragraphs. Ask students to paper-clip a transparency on top of the page. Have them use wipe-off markers to circle a specific paragraph on the transparency. Read the first sentence of the paragraph together, and then have students scan the page silently as you give directions for finding specific words and phrases. Give students prompts, such as *Find a word that means the opposite of tiny* or *Find a number word that begins with the /th/ sound.* Have students circle the words that match the clues. Share and discuss the answers. Continue the process with another paragraph and invite volunteers to give prompts to help classmates find key words and phrases.

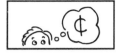 

Hieroglyphics

Materials

- overhead transparency and projector
- marker

Reading Strategies

▶ Using **context clues** to identify missing words

▶ Using **prior knowledge** to determine if sentences make sense

Write a simple paragraph pertaining to a current topic of study. Omit some of the key words and replace them with "hieroglyphics" (symbols). Make a transparency of the altered passage and use an overhead projector to show the text to students. Invite students to skip the "coded" words as they read the passage aloud. As students read, ask them questions about the text to check for comprehension. When students finish reading the entire passage, ask them to summarize what they have read. Discuss how they were able to understand the meaning of the passage, even with words missing, because of context clues.

Backtrack

Materials

- student reading materials
- chart paper and marker
- index cards
- scissors
- tape

Reading Strategies

▶ Using **prior knowledge** to add meaning to text

▶ Using **context clues** to identify unfamiliar words

In advance, copy on separate pieces of chart paper two different paragraphs from student reading materials. Leave enough space between the sentences in each paragraph to draw arrows above selected words. On the first paragraph, draw "U-turn" arrows above three or four key vocabulary words and draw straight arrows over a few other random words. Tape index-card strips over the arrows to make flip-up flaps. Discuss with students the importance of rereading a sentence when the meaning is not clear. Read together the first paragraph. When you reach a flip-up flap, invite a volunteer to lift the flap to show whether the class should continue reading (straight arrow) or backtrack and reread the sentence (U-turn arrow). After reading together the first paragraph, read the second, unmarked paragraph. This time, invite volunteers to draw the U-turn arrows to signal where it would be helpful to backtrack and reread the sentence.

Jackie rabbit was so happy! He was excited about the party.

Instant Replay

Materials

- student reading materials

Reading Strategies

▶ Using **prior knowledge** to add meaning to text

▶ Using **context clues** to identify unfamiliar words

In advance, copy a passage or a short story from student reading materials and underline key vocabulary words in the sentences. Make a photocopy of the marked passage for each student. Discuss the similarity between watching taped movies and reading a story. Explain that when reading a story, it is important to "rewind" and "fast forward" to review what has been read or to preview what's to come. Invite the class to read the passage aloud as you periodically call out *Rewind* or *Fast forward*. When you say *Rewind*, students are to go back and reread the sentence from the beginning. When you say *Fast forward*, they are to stop reading, write an *X* where they stopped, and then look ahead to preview the next underlined word. After discussing the meaning of the word, they are to go back to the *X* and continue reading where they left off. Have students read the entire passage, asking them to periodically reread a sentence or preview an underlined word. Share and discuss how these strategies help improve reading skills.

It's Time

Materials

- student reading books
- kitchen timer

Reading Strategies

▶ Using **prior knowledge** to add meaning to text

▶ Using **context clues** to identify unfamiliar words

Have the class read aloud a page from their reading book. After reading the page together, discuss with students the importance of rereading a section of a story when they encounter an unfamiliar word or when they do not understand what they are reading. Tell students they are to read the next page silently, but stop when they hear the timer. Explain that they must reread the last sentence before continuing on with the passage. Set the timer for a designated amount of time (one minute) and have students read the page. Reset the timer several times so that students reread many of the sentences before finishing the passage.

Computer Mix-Up

Materials

- two favorite storybooks
- overhead transparency and projector
- marker
- scissors
- glue
- construction paper

Reading Strategies

▶ Using **context clues** to determine the order of sentences in a paragraph

▶ Using rules of **grammar** to determine sentence sequence

▶ Using **prior knowledge** to determine if sentence sequence make sense

In advance, type a paragraph summary for each of two stories. Combine and retype the summaries together so that the two sets of sentences are intertwined, but the events in each story are still in correct order. Make an enlarged photo-copy of the revised summary for each pair of students. Make a transparency of the text and display it on an overhead projector. Explain to the class that the computer has mixed up sentences from two stories. Read together the jumbled text and challenge students to determine which sentences belong together so that each story looks right, sounds right, and makes sense. Invite partners to cut apart the sentences, sort them, and paste them together on construction paper so that each story is in proper sequence.

Variation: Have students mentally sort the sentences and rewrite each story in proper sequence.

The Three Little Pigs

There once lived three little pigs.

Goldilocks and the Three Bears

Papa bear said, "Who's been sleeping in my bed?"

Then the second little pig built a house of sticks.

Mama bear said, "Who's been sleeping in my bed?"

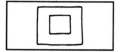 

Look-and-Listen Directories

Materials

- Look-and-Listen Directory sheet (page 109)

- construction paper

- stapler

- student reading materials or storybook

- crayons or colored pencils

Reading Strategies

▶ Looking at **letter patterns** to identify similar words

▶ Listening to **letter sounds** to identify and pronounce words

In advance, make a blank Look-and-Listen Directory for each student by stapling together photocopies of the Look-and-Listen Directory sheet. Make laminated construction-paper covers for the directories and then distribute the books to students. Have the class use the directories in one of two ways: to organize selected words in ABC order (each page represents a letter of the alphabet) or to list the words by book title (words from the same book are listed on one page). Ask students to write either letters of the alphabet or book titles at the top of each directory page. (continued)

Give students an example of how to use their Look-and-Listen Directories. Choose a word from students' reading materials, for example, the word *plant* from the story *Little Red Hen*. First have students write the word on the left side of the appropriate page, under the auditory cue—the ear illustration. Have them use a red crayon to underline the "key consonants" that are vital to sounding out the word, for example, *pl* and *nt* in plant.

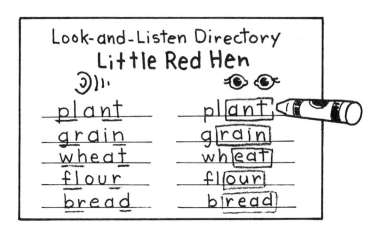

Then have students write the word on the right side of the page, under the visual cue—the eyes illustration. This time ask students to use a blue crayon to draw a box around any word they see "hidden" inside the word, for example *ant* in *plant*.

After the words have been reviewed and discussed (either one-on-one or as a class), invite the class to look for the words in their reading materials. Have students refer to their directories to remind themselves how to sound out and pronounce the words. Each week, have students add additional words to their directories.

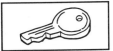 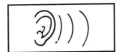 

Fun with Directories

Materials

- Look-and-Listen Directories

Reading Strategies

▶ Using **letter sounds** to pronounce and identify words

▶ Using **context clues** to identify words

▶ Using rules of **grammar** to spell words correctly

Encourage students to refer to their Look-and-Listen Directories as they participate in the following word games.

Mystery Word

Choose a "secret word" from the directory, a word that all students have in their books. Give students a clue to its identity by writing only the "key consonants"—no vowels—on the chalkboard. Invite students to sound out the letters to identify the word, and then have them find the word in their directory. Invite the student who correctly identifies the word first to fill in the missing letters on the chalkboard. Continue to play with other words. For an extra challenge, have students "beat the clock" as they find words in their directories. (continued)

Two-Second Race

Ask students to turn to a specific page in their directories. Tell students to scan the page and look for a specific word. After two seconds, say *Buzz!* to indicate time is up. Repeat this activity often to encourage scanning and "quick thinking" skills.

Clue

Ask students to find words in their directories using clues you say aloud. For example, you might say *On page 7, find a word that means "very big,"* or *On page 8, find the word that completes this sentence: The scared rabbit_____ away from the lion.*

The Nonsense Game

Say a sentence aloud that contains a "nonsense" word, for example, *The fox wanted to eat the "timtams."* Invite students to find a word in their directory that can be used in place of the nonsense word so the sentence makes sense. Tell students the page on which the word can be found. Challenge more advanced learners to find more than one "replacement" word to fit the sentence, for example, *apples, apricots,* and *avocados.* Use a sentence from a favorite storybook to offer students additional context clues to the identity of the nonsense word.

Roll a Word

Materials

- Word Families sheets (pages 91–93)
- dice
- sticky labels or dots
- marker
- writing paper
- chalkboard and chalk

Reading Strategies

▶ Pronouncing and combining **letter sounds** to form words

▶ Using **prior knowledge** to determine if words make sense

▶ Looking at **letter patterns** to identify similar words

In advance, cover the sides of dice with sticky labels or dots. Write different letter patterns (see Word Families, pages 91-93) on the sides of each die to make "pattern dice"—one die for each small group of students. Give each student a piece of paper and have him or her fold the paper in half lengthwise. Write five different consonant letters or clusters (for example, *b, d, g, tr,* and *str*) on the chalkboard, and have students copy them down the left side of their papers along the crease. Divide the class into small groups and give each group a pattern die. Have group members take turns rolling the dice and deciding which words can be formed by combining the pattern rolled with the letters on their papers. For example, students can combine the pattern *ad* to the letter *b* on their papers to form the word *bad.* Tell students they may only form one word (a real word, not a "nonsense" word) per turn. The member who completes his or her paper first wins.

A Phrase That Pays

Materials

- chalkboard and chalk
- three pairs of dice

Reading Strategies

▶ Using **context clues** to identify words

▶ Using **letter patterns** to combine letters into words

▶ Using **prior knowledge** to determine if words and phrases make sense

This activity is similar to the Wheel of Fortune game show, except students roll dice to earn points. In advance, select several words or phrases your students know well, such as animal names, movie characters, book titles, or popular sayings. Write on the chalkboard the category or clue for each word or phrase, and then write beside each clue fill-in-the-blank lines for each letter of the text. Divide the class into three teams, and have students take turns guessing the missing letters for each "puzzle," one puzzle at a time. Before team members begin guessing, have them roll the dice to determine how many points they'll earn for correct answers. For example, if a team member rolls a *3* and guesses a letter correctly, the team earns three points for every time that letter appears in the text. The team who guesses the puzzle correctly gets to keep the points, and the team with the most points at the end of the game wins.

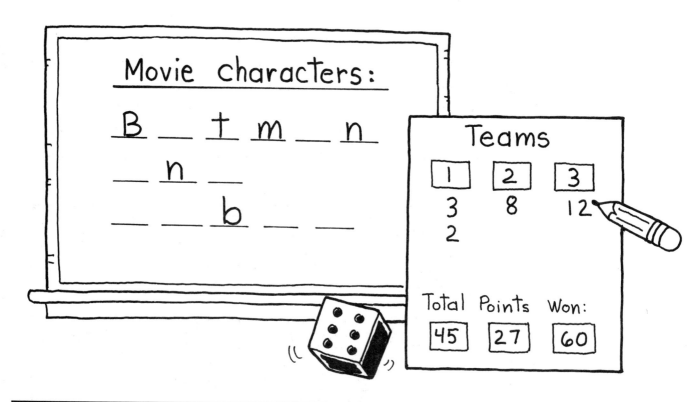

Culminating Activities

Use the following activities to encourage students to self-monitor and assess their use of reading strategies.

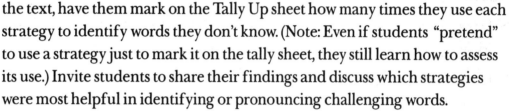

Tally Up

In advance, photocopy the Tally Up sheet (page 110) for each student. Ask the class to glance through a story and predict which strategies they will use most often. As students read the text, have them mark on the Tally Up sheet how many times they use each strategy to identify words they don't know. (Note: Even if students "pretend" to use a strategy just to mark it on the tally sheet, they still learn how to assess its use.) Invite students to share their findings and discuss which strategies were most helpful in identifying or pronouncing challenging words.

Strategy Wall

Post enlarged copies of the bookmark graphics on a bulletin board. When students use a specific reading strategy to identify a word they do not know, invite them to copy the sentence on a sentence strip, underline the challenging word, and attach the strip to the bulletin board under the corresponding graphic. Review the posted examples with the class. Discuss how different strategies can be used to identify the same word. To provide additional practice, use the bulletin board display as part of a learning center. Invite students to pull off posted examples, shuffle the paper strips, and reattach them to the display.

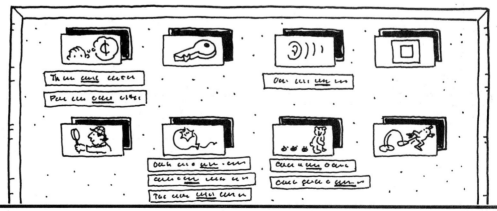

Strategy Graph

Use chart paper and photocopies of bookmark graphics to make an enlarged version of the Strategy Graph sheet (page 111). During guided reading, make a class bar graph to show which strategies are used most often to identify challenging words. Extend this to independent practice by making photocopies of the Strategy

Graph sheet and having students make their own bar graphs. Have students keep a list of the identified words on a separate piece of paper (or on index cards) and draw alongside each word the graphic of the strategy used.

Magnet Match

Photocopy and laminate bookmark graphics on colored paper. Tape magnet strips to the backs of pattern blocks. Cut and tape the bookmark graphics onto the different pattern blocks to make magnetic picture prompts for whole-class graphing activities on the chalkboard (or other magnetic surface). You can also use magnetic picture prompts with individual magnetic boards during small-group activities. For example, invite students to listen to incomplete lines of poems and fairy tales, and then ask them to place on magnetic boards the picture-prompt blocks that correspond to the reading strategies they used to identify the missing words.

Sneak a Peek

1. The title tells me _____

_____

2. The pictures tell me _____

_____

3. The setting of the story is _____

_____

4. The characters are _____

_____

5. The story is probably about _____

_____

Read a Rhyme

To Market, to Market

To market, to market
To buy a fat pig.
Home again, home again,
Jiggety-____ . (jig)

To market, to market
To buy a fat hog.
Home again, home again,
Jiggety-____ . (jog)

To market, to market
To buy a plum bun.
Home again, home again,
Market is ____ . (done)

One Misty, Moisty Morning

One misty, moisty morning
When cloudy was the weather,
I chanced to meet an old man
Clothed all in l____ r. (leather)

Clothed all in leather,
With a strap beneath his chin.
How do you do, and how do you do,
And how do you do a____ . (again)

Ding, Dong, Bell

Ding, dong, bell,
Pussy's in the ____ . (well)
Who put her in?
Little Johnny Green.

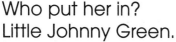

Who pulled her out?
Little Tommy S____ . (Stout)

What a naughty boy was that,
To try and drown poor pussy____ . (cat)

Who never did any harm,
And killed the mice on his father's f____ . (farm)

Reading Strategies That Work © 1998 Creative Teaching Press

Read a Rhyme

Little Jack Horner

Little Jack Horner
Sat in a _____ (corner)
Eating a Christmas pie.
He put in his thumb,
Pulled out a _____ , (plum)
And said, "What a good boy am I!"

There Was an Old Woman

There was an old woman
Lived under the hill,
And if she's not gone
She lives there __ ill. (still)

Rub a Dub Dub

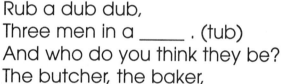

Rub a dub dub,
Three men in a _____ . (tub)
And who do you think they be?
The butcher, the baker,
The candlestick _____ ; (maker)
Turn 'em out, knaves all three!

Old Mother Hubbard

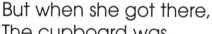

Old Mother Hubbard
Went to the cupboard
To fetch her poor _____ a bone. (dog)
But when she got there,
The cupboard was _____ , (bare)
And so the poor dog had none.

Hickety, Pickety, My Black Hen

Hickety, pickety, my black hen,
She lays eggs for gentle_____ . (men)
Gentlemen come every day
To see what my black hen doth lay.
Sometimes nine, sometimes _____ . (ten)
Hickety, pickety, my black hen.

Look Before You Leap

Reading Strategies That Work © 1998 Creative Teaching Press

Word Families—Short Vowels

-ack: back, jack, pack, rack, sack, tack, black, clack, crack, quack, shack, slack, snack, track

-ad: bad, dad, had, lad, mad, pad, sad, glad

-ag: bag, gag, lag, nag, rag, sag, tag, wag, drag, flag, shag, snag

-am: dam, ham, jam, ram, cram, slam, wham

-an: ban, can, fan, man, pan, ran, tan, van, plan, scan, hand, sand

-ap: cap, gap, lap, map, nap, rap, sap, tap, clap, flap, slap, snap, trap

-at: at, bat, cat, fat, hat, mat, pat, rat, sat, flat, that

-ed: bed, fed, led, red, wed, bred, fled, shed, sled, sped, shred

-ell: bell, cell, fell, sell, well, shell, smell, spell

-en: den, hen, men, pen, ten, then, when, wren

-est: best, jest, nest, rest, vest, west, chest, quest

-et: bet, get, jet, let, met, net, pet, set, vet, wet, yet, fret

-ick: kick, lick, pick, sick, tick, wick, brick, chick, quick, slick, stick, thick, trick

-id: did, hid, kid, lid, rid, slid, squid

-ig: big, dig, fig, jig, pig, rig, wig, twig

-ill: bill, dill, fill, gill, hill, mill, pill, sill, will, chill, drill, grill, frill, skill, spill, still, thrill

Word Families—Short Vowels

-in: fin, kin, pin, tin, win, chin, grin, skin, spin, thin, twin

-ing: king, ring, sing, wing, bring, cling, sling, sting, swing, spring, string, thing

-ink: link, mink, pink, rink, sink, wink, blink, drink, stink, think, shrink

-ip: dip, hip, nip, sip, tip, chip, slip, flip, drip, grip, trip, skip, ship, whip

-it: bit, fit, hit, kit, lit, pit, sit, wit, grit, knit, quit, slit, split, skit

-ock: dock, lock, knock, sock, rock, flock, shock, stock, clock, smock

-og: dog, clog, fog, hog, jog, log, frog, smog

-ot: cot, dot, hot, knot, lot, not, pot, rot, tot, plot, trot, spot

-op: drop, chop, hop, mop, pop, shop, stop, top

-ub: dub, cub, hub, rub, sub, club, grub, stub, scrub, shrub

-uck: buck, duck, luck, puck, tuck, chuck, cluck, stuck, truck, struck

-ug: bug, dug, drug, plug, hug, jug, mug, rug, tug, slug, snug

-um: bum, hum, gum, sum, drum, plum

-un: bun, fun, nun, pun, run, sun, spun

-ut: cut, nut, jut, rut, shut, strut

Reading Strategies That Work © 1998 Creative Teaching Press

Word Families—Long Vowels

-ail: bail, fail, hail, jail, mail, nail, pail, rail, sail, tail, wail, frail, snail, trail

-ain: gain, main, pain, rain, brain, chain, drain, grain, stain, train

-ake: bake, cake, lake, make, rake, take, wake, brake, shake, snake, stake

-ame: came, fame, game, lame, same, tame, blame, flame

-ank: bank, rank, sank, tank, blank, clank, crank, flank, plank, spank, thank

-ate: fate, gate, late, mate, plate, skate, state

-eat: eat, beat, heat, meat, neat, seat, treat, wheat

-eep: beep, deep, jeep, keep, peep, weep, creep, sheep, sleep, steep, sweep

-eet: feet, meet, sheet, sweet, sleet, street

-ice: ice, dice, lice, mice, nice, rice, price, slice, spice, twice

-ide: hide, ride, side, tide, wide, bride, glide, pride, slide

-ime: dime, lime, mime, time, crime, prime

-ive: dive, five, hive, live, drive

-oat: boat, coat, goat, bloat, float, gloat, throat

-old: bold, cold, gold, hold, mold, old, sold, told

-ole: hole, mole, pole, stole, whole

-one: bone, cone, tone, zone, phone, stone

-ose: hose, nose, rose, close, those

-y: by, my, cry, fly, fry, ply, sly, try, why

Name _____   Date _____

Mix and Match

Directions: Cut out the vowel squares. Place the vowel squares inside the blank boxes to form words. Rearrange the vowel squares to spell more words. How many different words can you spell?

h ☐ t	m ☐ p
s ☐ t	t ☐ p
h ☐ m	f ☐ n
b ☐ t	c ☐ b
d ☐ g	b ☐ d

a	e	i	o	u

I Spy

cat	did	lit	pop	set
kit	wet	jot	mug	vat
kid	dug	mit	rid	tub
ten	bat	lot	pen	fox
top	fit	pit	rot	tug
pet	get	met	sat	yet
wax	hug	net	pot	bit
pot	got	pat	rug	cot
cub	hat	men	rub	den
fat	hop	rat	sit	bet
bug	jet	not	tax	hit
hen	ax	mop	tot	jug

Reading Strategies That Work © 1998 Creative Teaching Press

Colorful Words

bit	slam
long	farm
drag	spill
star	bus
play	sink
mend	brain

Reading Strategies That Work © 1998 Creative Teaching Press

Colorful Words

small	shred
then	twin
glad	that
twig	harm
chart	stand
stop	band

Colorful Words

snap	flat
skit	chill
boxer	slip
plant	upset
think	about
grant	candy

Reading Strategies That Work © 1998 Creative Teaching Press

Alphabet Cards

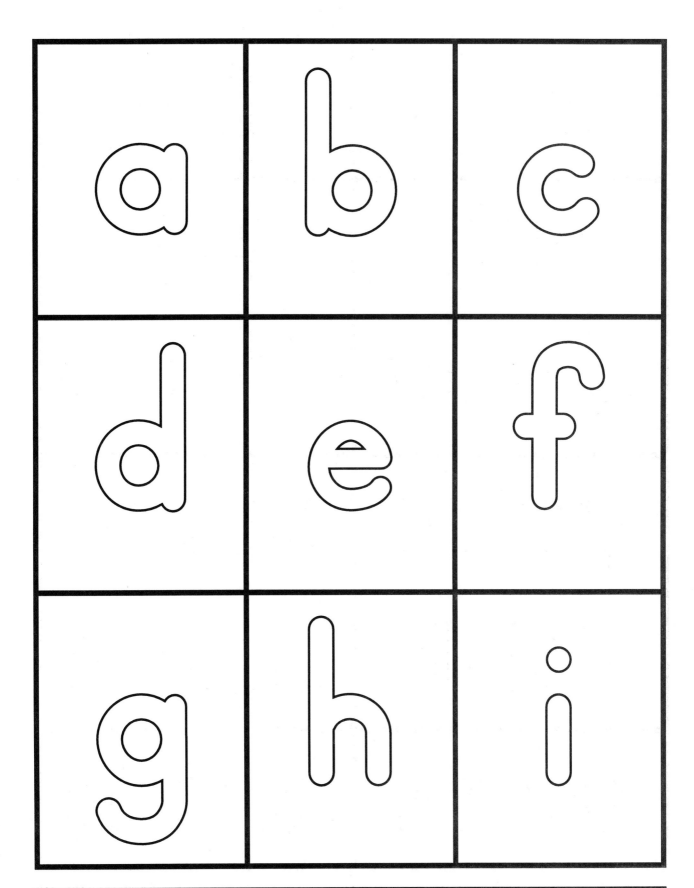

Alphabet Cards

j	k	l
m	n	o
p	q	r

Reading Strategies That Work © 1998 Creative Teaching Press

Alphabet Cards

s	t	u
v	w	x
y	z	

Scavenger Hunt

Hunt 1

pit	fin	sit	man	bat
and	ask	has	cat	kiss
his	fat	win	ran	bin

Hunt 2

mask	told	nice	your	knot
draw	fuse	ladder	blow	stone
know	fast	friend	plate	scold
shrink	train	struck	snail	twice
penny	pout	wheat	mother	candy
boat	bucket	spike	sweep	whole
knew	about	throw	relay	scare
smile	thumb	spring	bright	pride

Reading Strategies That Work © 1998 Creative Teaching Press

Letter Snatcher

1. Th__ d__g c__n gr__wl __t th__ c__t.

2. L__t's pl__y b__ll __t r__c__ss.

3. My fr____nd l__k__s t__ r__ller bl__d__.

4. W__ g__ t__ th__ st__r__ t__ g__t m__lk.

5. Th__ r__bb__t h__ps __n th__ gr__ss.

6. Sh__ w__nt t__ th__ b__s__b__ll g__m__.

7. Th__ l__ttl__ k__tt__n w__s l__st.

8. Th__ cl____ds __r__ b__g __nd wh__t__.

The Attribute Game

Grid 1

	red	green	blue
food			
outside			
animal			

Grid 2

	A	B	C
food			
outside			
animal			

Grid 3

	T	M	R
boy's name			
girl's name			
pet			

Reading Strategies That Work © 1998 Creative Teaching Press

Word Translator

Telephone Spelling

Reading Strategies That Work © 1998 Creative Teaching Press

Try-ers

Part I: Vowel Combinations

Directions: Decide which vowel combination to use as you read each sentence aloud.

<u>Think about It</u>   <u>Try It</u>

1. /ow/ as in *low* or /ow/ as in *clown?*   I put a bow in my hair.

2. /oo/ as in *book* or /oo/ as in *moon?*   The cook make a cake.

3. /ea/ as in *head* or /ea/ as in *bead?*   She wore a cap on her head.

Part II: Vowel Discrimination

Directions: Choose the word that best completes each sentence.

1. The wind blew the tall _____ (pin/pine) tree.

2. The water in the _____ (tub/tube) was cold.

3. He wore a red baseball _____ (cap/cape).

4. It will cost a _____ (dim/dime) to call home.

5. The rabbits like to _____ (hop/hope) in their cage.

6. Susie and _____ (Pet/Pete) went to the park.

Shift and Change

Directions: Have students build words using letter cards as you read the following directions aloud. Offer prompts when needed. Letters needed for this lesson: *t, a, n, i, g, s*

Take two letters and make the word *it.*

Now change one letter to make the word *at.*

Add one letter to make the word *ant.*

Without adding or taking away any letters, see if you can make a new word. (Tell younger students the word—*tan.*)

Now change one letter and rearrange others to make the word *sat.*

Change just one letter to make the word *sag.*

Once again, without adding or taking away letters, see if you can make a new word. (Tell younger students the word—*gas.*)

Now take away the *s* and the *a*, leaving only the *g,* and add two letters to make the ending sound –*ing.*

Now add another letter to make the word *sing.*

Add one more letter to make the word *sting.*

Take the *g* away, and add another letter to make the word *stain.* (Tell students they will need to move one letter to a new spot.)

Move the letters around to make a new word. (Tell younger students the word—*saint.*)

Now that we've made these different words, can anyone make a word that uses all six letters? Here are some clues: It's something really, really big, and it has the word *ant* in it.

(Answer: *giants*)

Reading Strategies That Work © 1998 Creative Teaching Press

Look-and-Listen Directory

_____
(alphabet letter or book title)

_____   _____

_____   _____

_____   _____

_____   _____

_____   _____

✂ --

Look-and-Listen Directory

_____
(alphabet letter or book title)

_____   _____

_____   _____

_____   _____

_____   _____

_____   _____

Tally Up

Strategy Graph

Notes